Seraph**Creative**

Heaven's Heart for Earth

New Christmas

Written by Joey LeTourneau

Illustrations created by Galilee LeTourneau using MidJourney AI

Published by Seraph Creative in 2024

United States / United Kingdom / South Africa / Australia

www.seraphcreative.org

I

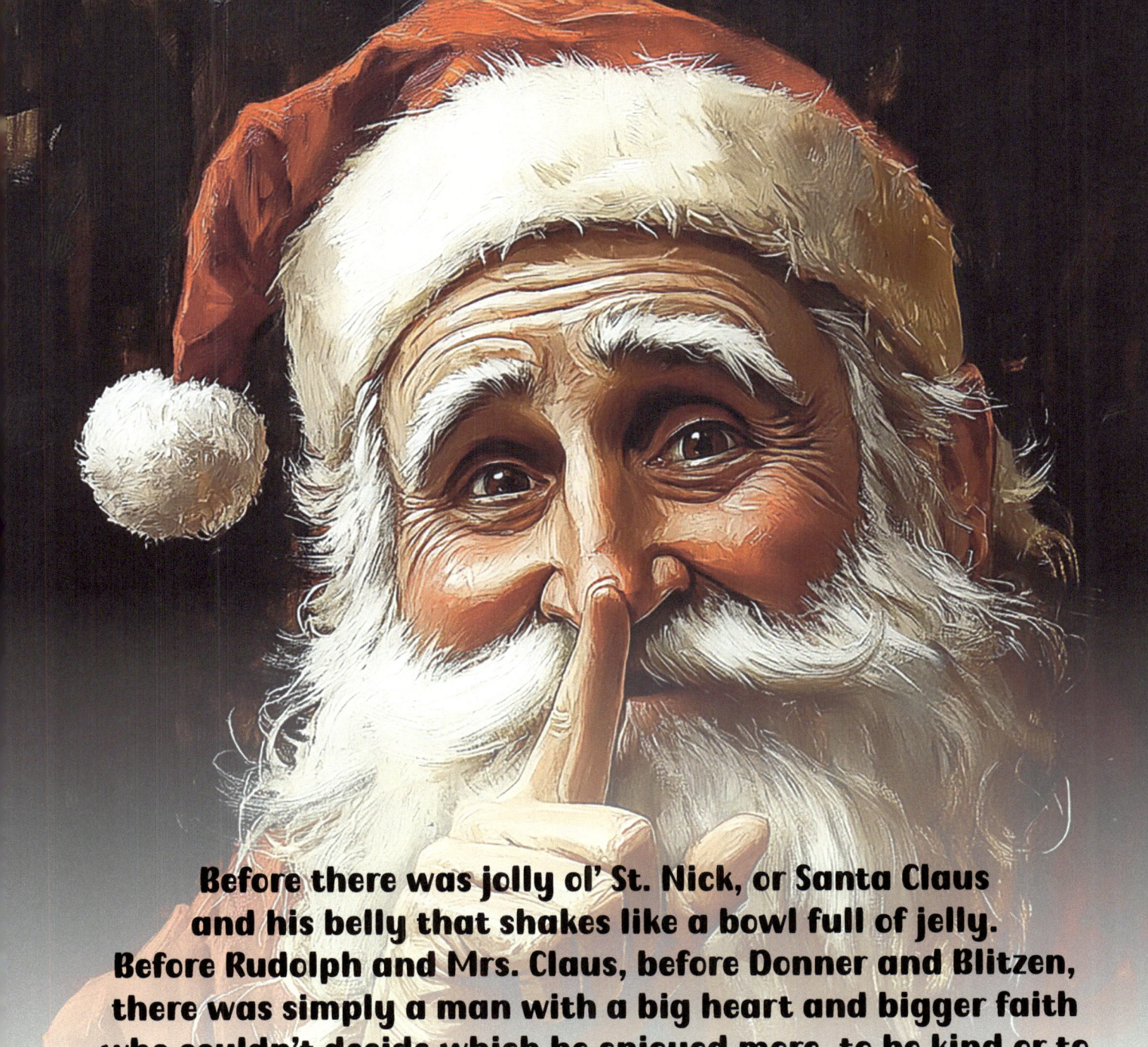

Before there was jolly ol' St. Nick, or Santa Claus
and his belly that shakes like a bowl full of jelly.
Before Rudolph and Mrs. Claus, before Donner and Blitzen,
there was simply a man with a big heart and bigger faith
who couldn't decide which he enjoyed more, to be kind or to
be generous? So he decided to be both!

Before Christmas became the worldwide phenomenon and shopping season that we know today, St. Nicholas began what we now call Christmas with a very special list of his own. His account was a chart of those in his community who needed help or perhaps those who needed hope. From the start, he loved to give surprising, secret gifts to those in need.

One year, some months before Christmas, St. Nicholas realized it had been quite the many years since he had done a thorough audit on how his beloved holiday was going in the world, among all the people he cared about so much.

Sure, he had made plenty of other visits to help usher in Christmas spirit and make sure gifts were given, carols were sung, and of course, that cookies and milk were always eaten! But it was time he looked beyond the naughty or nice list, and instead, looked at the bigger picture of what first motivated his extravagant giving.

St. Nicholas was barely beginning his Christmas research when he realized that most of the poor in the world, those to whom his secret giving was originally meant, were barely being celebrated or redeemed at all. Their lives weren't being turned upside down by those who had the ability to help do so. Instead, his favorite holiday had become little more than endless lists of personal wants, instead of the thoughtful, generous giving that could change a life or a family.

Now please understand, St. Nicholas loved the gifts, and he loved to bring joy to every child and family! He didn't want to change that part. And he saw that many people did still carry out the spirit of how it all began. But if there were more who thought and lived that way, well, then Christmas could perhaps change the world once again!

13

St. Nicholas thought long and hard about what to do. He consulted with the elves, and when they still couldn't come up with a new plan that was both big and yet simple enough to make Christmas what it should be, he retired to home, feeling sad, for a quiet evening. And before he drank his milk and ate his cookies, he got down on his knees to pray. "Dear heavenly Father, I need your help. I am honored by this holiday, and I love the presents and the giving, but I fear my mission has failed. Gifts are indeed being given, but the spirit of Christmas is not being felt by those who truly need it most. Forgive me. And please help me. Amen."

Later that night, when St. Nicholas was fast asleep, an angel snuck quietly into his room the way he might normally sneak down chimneys and into homes. The angel was sure to say nothing, but left in St. Nicholas' open hand a single, handwritten scroll.

Early that next morning, St. Nicholas began to stir and awoke to find this tied up scroll grasped loosely in his hand. His eyes got big, and a holy excitement filled him again like he hadn't felt in years! He opened the scroll and nodded along as he read what was the answer to his prayers.

The New Christmas Scroll read…This Christmas, I, St. Nicholas, would like to proclaim a new method to your holiday that many celebrate with my name. There was and is another who provoked my first venture of gifts, and loving others was one of the two greatest commandments on His list. Not only that, but often did He say, what you do for the poor or hurting is what you have done unto Me. That's where I started and to there we must together return, only then will kids and families across the world experience the love for which they all naturally yearn. So, on this day, this Christmas year and onward, I will still visit you, but only as you're generous with someone who is in need and also with someone who is new. Those two gifts should start your family's season, a surprise to someone you don't know and a gift to those who need it most!   Signed, Your Beloved Friend, St. Nicholas

Now, what was he to do? He and the elves went quickly to work, writing and producing as fast as they could; one handmade copy of this New Christmas Scroll to be delivered to every family and person around the whole world.

The day after Thanksgiving, on a day that many now call black, St. Nicholas decided to pay each house an early visit, and every home would receive that New Christmas Scroll; guidelines that he hoped would revive the holiday to be what he had intended since the beginning. It would no longer be about his naughty and nice list, for that part would take care of itself if every family across the world paused their lists long enough to start their season by giving to those who needed it most.

The next morning, each family began to wake up, not yet knowing they were about to get a big pre-Christmas surprise from St. Nicholas himself. And honestly, their hearts might not yet have been ready.

Many people, all around the world were awestruck to find this early Christmas delivery from the man himself, let alone such a message that was not in the form of a gift they might have expected. And as the people read them, St. Nicholas and his elves watched from out of sight, hoping New Christmas would tilt the world back towards what he truly believed was right.

However, as the people first read the scroll that was left on their door, while a few nodded in agreement and some even rejoiced; wouldn't you know, others threw tantrums, and quite a few shook their heads in disgust as they were thinking about "me" and not about "us." Some even wadded up the scroll to throw it in the trash so they could continue to go about Christmas the way they wanted and planned.

But as the days passed, Christmas was drawing near, parents and families returned to the scroll, and little by little they started to see things even a bit more clear. While many still wondered silently or aloud, "Who on earth wants a Christmas that is new?" Many started to realize, "Well, boys, girls and families all around the world, that's who!" But honestly, they still didn't know what to do.

St. Nicholas was aware of how hard change can be for so much of the world, especially involving a beloved holiday and the patterns that many held dear. Yet, he believed his Christmas reformation would restore his true reason for the season, and he just needed a little jumpstart to help lead that new way.

He sent an army of elves to watch as the big day approached, not for who is naughty or nice, but to see who would listen, and who might start to bring his New Christmas Scroll to life.

They didn't wear their typical red or green, and their pointy hats were retired for the moment, or so it seemed. The elves did their best to scatter and find places to blend in, despite their tiny size and, ahem, little elf ears that stood out and defined them.

The elves found many places to hide and spy. They hid in trees. They rode secretly in cars. Many slept in stockings and even more enjoyed the sweet nights of a cookie jar.

And apparently, one elf hid in a suitcase that must have taken him away long and far.

But the mission had to go on. St. Nicholas needed the help of the people to bring his holiday back to where it began; secret, generous giving to those who needed it most.

The elves returned some days before Christmas with a startling report. They recorded that perhaps only a handful of families were living out St. Nicholas' new Christmas hope. And pretty certain were they that most of those were ones who already lived the scrolls principles on their own. So, unfortunately, there had been little to no change at all.

They needed another plan—and quickly! The scroll by itself was not enough. It would take a special kind of help to bring this "New Christmas" movement to life. It was the only way to see the hurt on so many unseen children's faces made right.

That's when St. Nicholas' face perked up and he jumped up with a shout! "Who have we always been able to trust at Christmas when we needed it most?" The elves murmured to one another about this person or that, but still unsure of who their fearless leader was speaking about with such clear intent.

"The kids!" If the adults and parents of the world won't bring in this change, I believe we can trust the children to make Christmas love and generosity grow once more, to all of the nations of the earth, or so he hoped.

43

Now, just days before Christmas, they all went back to work. They weren't making toys or packing any sleighs (yet!). They were re-printing the New Christmas Scrolls; but this time, these scrolls would be given to those they could trust the most, the children.

He gathered every elf and they held a pre-Christmas rally, where he gave them their new mission to search all sides of the earth.

Wherever there was a child, just as the angel had done that night for St. Nicholas, the elves were to leave one New Christmas Scroll in each child's hand while they slept.

However, this time, for clarity's sake, the scrolls were written in crayon just to make sure every child would truly heed and understand.

New Christmas

St. Nicholas waited while the elves made this delivery. He
tapped his feet and twiddled his fingers like an anxious child on
Christmas morning. What would become of this holiday he held
so dear? It would now be in the hands of beloved
kids from everywhere.

Every scroll was delivered before the kids could even blink an eye. And wouldn't you know it, the first child opened her scroll, looked around the room with awestruck wonder, unable to believe she had been handpicked for this mission by St. Nicholas himself.

The second child and third, a whole continent away, responded almost exactly the same. Holy fear and hopeful joy came over them as well, the same kind that St. Nicholas once felt when his loving generosity launched this holiday that first night.

Their awe became action, and the kids jumped to attention. They walked past their own Christmas lists to see what they might have in their hands to share. "Someone new, and someone needy!" One child yelled with glee. He woke his mother and father to help him prepare a gift for each.

And, of course, like all of the others, his mom and dad, not long ago, already saw the New Christmas Scroll, which they, too, had ignored. At first, they felt guilty for the lack of love they showed, but then quickly became proud of their son for his obvious heart of gold.

And while parents still bought gifts of joy for their kids and families, and others offered presents to those they loved; because of how the children freely led them, everyone participated in St. Nicholas' new mission of holiday hope.

NEW CHRISTMAS HAD BEGUN!

Like a freshly unwrapped game of dominoes from under the tree, the giving became contagious and spread as one after another, the kids and their families bought generous, surprising gifts for those they didn't yet know, and extra special gifts for those in need.

Across the world, from Argentina, to Cambodia, to Mozambique!
Children who had never gotten presents before were suddenly
blessed by that generous, unstoppable dominoes train of
giving that went further than the eye could see.

St. Nicholas sat in his chair and cried with a most wonderful smile! Christmas is saved, it's new again, it now looks much more like that manger with that Child.

So here we are with Christmas once again right around the corner. And St. Nicholas is hoping that the adults too, will return to the faith and generosity of the children who now lead them.

What will you do? Where will you go, and how will you give? Can you see beyond your lists and into the hearts of those who Christmas has too long missed? Just two thoughtful gifts, that's all St. Nicholas asks. One for someone new, who might need a redemptive surprise. And one for those in need because they, too, deserve to have new hope in their eyes.

MERRY CHRISTMAS TO ALL, AND TO ALL A NEW CHRISTMAS SCROLL THIS NIGHT!

Joey and his wife, Destiny, have been married for 23 years. They have eight children and two grandchildren. As a family, they have both lived, and traveled, all around the world, empowering people to discover and live out who they were created to be. Joey has authored eleven books, and three children's books. As a family, they write and create to give life to a generation who will shine in the world.

To see other books and projects by the author, please visit: LeTourneau Creative

LeTourneau
Creative

LeTourneaucreative.com

New Christmas: Give to Someone New Or in Need

This Christmas, we invite you to embrace the true spirit of giving by reaching out to someone new or in need. Your generosity will directly impact the lives of children in Cambodia, Uganda, Ethiopia, Mozambique, and Ukraine—places where our nonprofit is working tirelessly to bring hope and a brighter future.

With your support, we can provide essential resources, education, and opportunities to children who need it most. Every donation, no matter the size, makes a significant difference.

Where Your Donation Goes:

- **Uganda:** Providing essential supplies and care for vulnerable children.
- **Ethiopia:** Empowering youth with access to education and resources.
- **Mozambique:** Offering support to children affected by poverty and hardship.
- **Cambodia:** Supporting children through our Cambodia Kidz programs at Esther's House (a rescue home for underage girls), Joshua House, and OCTO (both homes for orphaned and vulnerable children).
- **Ukraine:** Delivering relief and hope to children in crisis.

We are deeply grateful for your kindness and commitment to making the world a better place. Together, we are spreading hope and love this Christmas season.

TOGETHER WE CAN MAKE A DIFFERENCE

Seraph Creative is a collective of artists, writers, theologians & illustrators who desire to see the body of Christ grow into full maturity, walking in their inheritance as Sons of God on the Earth.

Sign up to our newsletter to know about future exciting releases.

Visit our website: www.seraphcreative.org